GOODNESS
GRACIOUS

**30 DEVOTIONS ON ALLOWING GOODNESS
AND GRACE TO LEAD US TO HOLINESS**

ISBN 978-1-0877-4437-7
Item 005831825
Dewey Decimal Classification Number: 242
Subject Heading: DEVOTIONAL LITERATURE / BIBLE STUDY AND TEACHING / GOD

Printed in the United States of America

Student Ministry Publishing
Lifeway Resources
One Lifeway Plaza
Nashville, Tennessee 37234

We believe that the Bible has God for its author; salvation for its end; and truth, without any mixture of error, for its matter and that all Scripture is totally true and trustworthy. To review Lifeway's doctrinal guideline, please visit www.lifeway.com/doctrinalguideline.

publishing team

Director, Student Ministry
BEN TRUEBLOOD

Manager, Student Ministry Publishing
JOHN PAUL BASHAM

Editorial Team Leader
KAREN DANIEL

Writer
MIKE LOVATO

Content Editor
STEPHANIE CROSS

Production Editor
BROOKE HILL

Graphic Designer
JON RODDA

table of contents

Intro

If you were asked to define what's good, what would you say? Would you point to vibrant sunshine and say it's a good day? Would you point to the girl who listened as you spilled your thoughts and feelings about the guy who broke your heart? Or would you point to a sweet, adorable, and obedient dog? While we might define these things as good, we have to know where good comes from. After all, to indicate something as good, there has to be some sort of standard. Right?

The world we live in—despite its flaws and its sin-damaged image—still has beauty. And that beauty, that good, calls us to look for a source. While it can seem difficult at times to see how the truly good things in our lives point to God, Scripture makes it clear that *every* good and perfect thing is a gift from Him. So, when we begin to trace the good around us back to its source, our search will lead us straight to God.

The only real standard for goodness comes straight from God the Father—the Father of all creation; the Father who is unchanging and eternal; the Father whose very character is good; the Father who gives us standards in His Word, by which we may know what's good and what isn't. We have to begin with Him to begin defining what good really is.

While that might seem like a daunting task, God has given us His Son, His Spirit, and His Word to help us understand what's good. With His help and guidance, over the next 30 days, we'll seek to answer these key questions about what's good:

- What is goodness, really?

- Are people naturally good?

- What does goodness look like?

- What does God say is good?

Follow along as we pursue the goodness of our gracious God and learn to live in it and live it out every single day.

getting started

This devotional contains 30 days of content, broken down into sections about God's goodness. Each day is divided into three elements—discover, delight, and display—to help you answer core questions related to Scripture.

discover

This section helps you examine the passage in light of who God is and determine what it says about your identity in relationship to Him. Included here is the daily Scripture reading, focus passage, along with illustrations and commentary to guide you as you explore God's Word.

delight

In this section, you'll be challenged by questions and activities that help you see how God is alive and active in every detail of His Word and your life.

display

Here's where you take action. Display calls you to apply what you've learned through each day's study.

prayer

Each day also includes a prayer activity in one of the three main sections.

Throughout the devotional, you'll also find extra articles and activities to help you connect with the topic personally, such as such as Scripture memory verses, additional resources, and questions.

GOOD FRUIT

- -

discover |

READ GALATIANS 5:22-23.

But the fruit of the Spirit is love, joy, peace, patience, kindness, goodness, faithfulness, gentleness, and self-control. The law is not against such things.

The people God used to write Scripture often used language from nature and agriculture. Picture an apple tree in your mind and imagine what its fruit looks like. They look like apples, right? You'd never go to an orange grove to pick apples.

As Paul wrote to the Christians in Galatia, he described the type of fruit that results from walking in the Spirit. He listed nine qualities that come from being led by the Holy Spirit. An apple tree will produce apples if it's in the right environment (with the right temperature and the right type of soil) and has the right resources (sunlight and water). Christians produce the fruit of the Spirit when they place themselves in the right environment (fellowship with God and believers) and have the right resources (Bible intake, prayer, and other disciplines).

Let's zero in on just one fruit mentioned in this passage: goodness. The type of goodness mentioned here is moral and spiritual excellence. Goodness shows up in our lives when we choose to slow down and meet the need of a girl who is hurting. Goodness is on display when we reflect God's character by the attitude we show our family members.

The reality is, we can only see this type of moral and spiritual excellence in our lives because of the new life we have in Jesus. Today, focus on how the fruit of goodness is visible to those you're around each day.

delight |

How have you seen your Christian friends live out goodness?

How have you seen the Holy Spirit developing goodness as part of His fruit in your life?

display |

Goodness is a quality that has to be lived out. You can't just focus on goodness being present on the inside. Ask yourself a tough question: *Would most of my friends describe goodness as a characteristic of my life?* After reflecting on that question, take some time this week to intentionally pursue goodness in the way you treat different people in your life. You might seek to pursue goodness with your teachers, your parents, or maybe a girl at school who's difficult to get along with.

> Take a few minutes to pray. Ask God to reveal to you the areas of your life where goodness is lacking. Pray that He would begin transforming those areas of your life. Don't worry about accomplishing this through your own efforts. Instead, focus on walking in the Spirit to allow Him to produce this fruit in you.

DAY 2

DEFINER OF GOODNESS

- -

discover |

READ 1 CHRONICLES 16:34.

Give thanks to the LORD, for he is good; his faithful love endures forever.

What makes someone good? Maybe you've seen a girl pick up trash after lunch, befriend another girl everyone else avoids, or help her grandma with housework. It may seem easy to define goodness, but to fully understand it, we must get to the core of where goodness comes from.

Yesterday, we talked about how goodness is moral and spiritual excellence. The reality is, there is only One being who can determine what is truly good. God is the essence of goodness. He gets to define goodness because He's both Creator and the only One in the universe who is fully good. Without God, there is no good. Any goodness accomplished by people points to the truth that there is indeed a Creator. Humans reflect just a glimpse of the goodness found in Him.

First Chronicles 16:34 is a portion of King David's song of praise, which he commanded to be sung after the ark of the covenant had been returned to Jerusalem following the defeat of the Philistines. David's exuberant thanksgiving flowed from a place of recognizing God's goodness.

It's reassuring to not only know that God commands goodness to be displayed in His followers, but to also realize goodness is an essential part of God's character. He can only do good; He will never commit evil. Dwell on the reality today that God is good all the way to the very center of who He is.

---

delight |

Why is it such a big deal that God is the ultimate Author of goodness?

Imagine for a moment if God was not truly good. How would that affect other aspects of the Christian faith?

display |

Think for about how you've viewed goodness in the world we live in. Maybe you've somehow mentally separated the good deeds people do from the One who gave them the ability to accomplish them. Ask the Holy Spirit to guide you as you search your heart: Have you defined goodness by popular opinion or by God's character?

Focus your attention today on our God who defines goodness simply because of who He is. He is worthy of your praise and adoration. Read about the attributes of God at https://www.blueletterbible.org/faq/attributes.cfm. Focus in on different aspects of God's character. Write out each of these attributes in a journal or on a blank sheet of paper. His goodness is in everything He has done. How do you see His goodness in each of these attributes? How have you seen His goodness in your life?

> Stop for a moment and praise God for His goodness. First, praise Him because He is good. Then, thank Him specifically for the ways you've seen Him be good in your life or the lives of others you know. Pray that you would seek to have a heart that looks like His.

DAY 3

GOOD GIFTS

- -

discover |

READ JAMES 1:13-18.

Every good and perfect gift is from above, coming down from the
Father of lights, who does not change like shifting shadows.
—James 1:17

We all like to play the blame game. Have you ever said something
ugly to or about another girl because she hurt you? Our typical
response when confronted about our actions is: "But she started
it!" Sound familiar? Humans have been playing the blame game
since the very beginning. In the garden of Eden, Adam blamed Eve
and Eve blamed the serpent for their disobedience (Gen. 3:12-13).

We still play this blame game today. It's tough to own up to what
you've done! Sometimes you may even be tempted to blame God
for the times we choose to do evil. James quickly tears this idea
down in the first chapter of his letter. It's impossible for God to
tempt you. Why? Because God isn't tempted by evil and doesn't
tempt anyone else with evil. He is one hundred percent good
without any mix of evil. God's character will never allow for this
type of temptation to come from Him.

James contrasts this with a much better truth: Every good thing
comes from God. Evil is not from God; He brings every good thing
into our lives. The difficult truth is that we're the ones to blame
when we choose to sin. The desire comes from within. Today, let
go of any blame you may be holding onto and instead choose to
receive the good gifts coming from the Father.

delight |

Do you ever find yourself thinking that maybe God is tempting you with evil? Why or why not?

What are some ways you've played the blame game when it comes to sin in your life?

display |

Owning up to our own shortcomings, mistakes, and sins is one of the most freeing things in life. The reality is, you'll never be perfect until you reach heaven, so there's no point in trying to play the blame game. You might want to blame God, your friends, or your circumstances. But at the end of the day, the only one to blame for your sin is yourself.

When we own up to what we've done, we experience the refreshment of forgiveness only Jesus can offer. Choose today to let go of sin and blame. Walk in freedom instead. If you've been blaming someone else for sin in your life, take responsibility for your own actions.

Who have you blamed recently for something you know you did? Prayerfully consider going to that person and seeking forgiveness.

Reflect on your heart for a few minutes. Ask God to reveal any areas of sin or blame that you may be holding on to. Release those areas to Him as you turn from them and receive forgiveness in their place.

SAVED FOR GOOD WORKS

- -

discover |

READ EPHESIANS 2:1-10.

For you are saved by grace through faith, and this is not from yourselves; it is God's gift—not from works, so that no one can boast. For we are his workmanship, created in Christ Jesus for good works, which God prepared ahead of time for us to do.
—Ephesians 2:8-10

You cannot be good on your own. In fact, the apostle Paul wrote to a church in a city called Ephesus to tell them they were dead before Christ. There is no possible way for a person who is dead to be good.

Fortunately for us, Christ has taken spiritually dead people and brought them to life. Jesus brings about the ability for goodness to be present in our lives. It's all because of God's grace, which is activated by our faith—simply placing our trust in what Jesus has done and choosing to follow Him.

There is no amount of good behavior on your part that will move you from being spiritually dead to alive. It is purely a gift from God. If good works saved you, every Christian would end up in a bragging contest about the good things they did to earn salvation.

We are not saved by good works, but we are saved for good works. God saved you so that you can now live in a way that brings goodness into the world all around you.

delight |

What is the difference between saved by good works and being saved for good works?

Why do you think some people believe their goodness can save them?

display |

It's really great news that your goodness doesn't save you. You could never be good enough! Even though we know this truth, sometimes we may find ourselves slipping back into a mode of thinking that it's somehow our goodness that keeps us in a right relationship with God. Ask yourself this question: *Am I relying on my goodness to save me or am I relying on Jesus to save me?*

Cling to the reality that Jesus has accomplished the act of bringing goodness into your life. He sees you as His workmanship. Use a dry-erase marker to write out on your mirror: *You're an incredible work of art that He's creating to display His goodness.* Let this serve as a reminder for you to choose to live out the good works He's saved you for.

> **Pause for a moment in prayer. Thank God for saving you by grace and not because of any goodness you've been able to accomplish. Praise Him that He has brought you from death to life. Ask Him to show you the good works He's calling you to right now.**

TASTE OF GOODNESS

- -

discover |

READ PSALM 34:8-10.

*Taste and see that the Lord is good. How happy
is the person who takes refuge in Him!*
—Psalm 34:8

Think about the most exciting place you've ever visited. You
probably researched the best coffee shops, boutiques, restaurants,
and sights. You couldn't wait to get there and start exploring. You
knew the place was beautiful and that you'd have fun. But, be
honest, you had no idea just how amazing this place was until you
arrived, right?

There are some things you can only truly discover by experience.
It may be a delicious meal, a view of the mountains, or the breeze
of the ocean. You may think you understand by a description or
picture, but only experience brings true understanding.

God's goodness is like that. You can read about God's goodness
or hear people share their stories of God's goodness. But until you
experience it for yourself, you don't truly comprehend it. One small
taste of God's goodness leaves you with the reality of how good
He truly is.

Your first glimpse of your favorite place likely left you wanting to
experience even more of this magical place. But those who taste
of God's goodness end up having everything they need and more.
Think about the small tastes of God's goodness you've experienced
and how they can shape your actions today.

delight |

What are some ways you've tasted God's goodness?

Have you ever tasted God's goodness but still lived as if you hadn't? Why or why not?

display |

The psalmist went on to mention two key actions we ought to embrace once we've tasted the Lord's goodness. First, we are to fear Him. This essentially means to take God seriously. Second, we are to seek Him. This indicates an intentional pursuit that we put effort into. Hopefully, you've gotten a taste of God's goodness.

On a scale of 1-10, how seriously do you take God, His Word, and His call on your life?

1   2   3   4   5   6   7   8   9   10

Now, reflect on and list the actions you're currently taking to seek God. The taste of God's goodness is motivation to pursue Him with your whole heart.

In your time of prayer, ask God to give you a fresh taste of His goodness today. Ask Him to show you clearly how He's bringing good things into your life. Take time as you pray to engage with God in a serious way that shows your desire to seek Him in every area of your life.

DAY 6

GOD'S GENEROSITY

- -

discover |

READ MATTHEW 20:1-16.

*Don't I have the right to do what I want with what
is mine? Are you jealous because I'm generous?*
—Matthew 20:15

"It's not fair." Most of us learned how to use this phrase pretty early in life. We hate it when it seems like someone else is benefiting and we think it ought to be us. Jesus used the parable of the vineyard workers to display how the distribution of God's goodness and generosity is up to Him alone. The workers hired first believed they ought to be paid higher wages than those who worked less, even though they had agreed upon an amount of pay at the start of the day.

Jealousy of God's goodness has no place in the life of a believer. Ultimately, God gives the same gift of salvation to all who come to Him in faith, no matter when or how that happens. You might find yourself tempted to be jealous when observing a new believer's influence, giftedness, or perceived blessings. We can fight this type of jealousy by reminding ourselves that the decision to give good things to people comes from God alone.

If you hold on to this type of jealousy, there's a scary lie you're believing: the lie that you know better than God. God alone saves people. God alone blesses people. And God alone decides what He gives to His children. Today, reject the lie that you know better than God and embrace a grateful heart for all the goodness He has brought to you.

delight |

Why do you think it bothered the workers in the parable that the people hired later got paid the same wage?

Have you ever found yourself jealous of the blessings God has given to someone else? If so, why?

display |

Jealousy is an easy sin to slide into. At our very core, we are constantly telling ourselves a message that says, "I deserve better." What would it look like if, instead of jealousy, you decided to live gratefully because of the incredible gift of salvation God has given you? God's goodness is on display as He decides to generously dispense His goodness.

Responding with gratitude requires making the decision to set aside jealous thoughts and being grateful for the brothers and sisters God has brought into His family in different ways. In a journal or on a sheet of paper, write out the names of girls you most often feel jealous of. Beside their names, write out at least one reason you're grateful for them instead.

Spend a few moments in a prayer of gratitude. Thank God specifically for the ways He has shown His goodness to you. Thank Him for His goodness of both His character and His actions. Thank Him for the other Christians you know and the ways He has drawn them into a relationship with Himself.

For you are saved by grace through faith, and this is not from yourselves; it is God's gift—not from works, so that no one can boast.

For we are his workmanship, created in Christ Jesus for good works, which God prepared ahead of time for us to do.

EPHESIANS 2:8-10

NO ONE IS GOOD

- -

discover |

READ ROMANS 3:9-20.

As it is written: There is no one righteous, not even one.
There is no one who understands; there is no one who seeks
God. All have turned away; all alike have become worthless.
There is no one who does what is good, not even one.
—Romans 3:10–12

Picture the meanest girl you know. Think about the way she treats others and how she lives. Now, picture the nicest girl you know. Consider her behavior toward other people. Do you know what these two girls have in common? Neither of them are truly good. The Bible tells us that no one is righteous, not even the girl who seems good by our human standards. (We'll talk more about this tomorrow.)

Goodness is a fruit of the Spirit. The only way for goodness to truly be in our lives is through the Holy Spirit's work. Apart from this, we constantly turn to our own evil desires and don't produce the goodness God desires. The human condition, ever since Adam and Eve first sinned, is one of sinfulness and evil.

But the recognition of this bad news is what makes the gospel truly good news. Our inability to be good on our own highlights the incredible work of God as He makes us righteous and good through Jesus. Allow yourself to sit with the weight of our lack of goodness apart from God's work.

delight |

As you look through today's passage, what thoughts or emotions come to your mind and heart?

If no one is good, how can anyone ever come into a relationship with God?

display |

It's normal to want to think of yourself as better than you really are. No one wants to focus on the bad things they do, the dark desires in their hearts, or the tempting thoughts they have. But the Bible makes it clear that none of us are truly good at our core.

Maybe you need to allow the Holy Spirit to begin transforming your life by placing your trust in Jesus for the first time. Or maybe your next move is seeking to walk in step with the Spirit, allowing Him to produce goodness in your life. Either way, consider talking about your next steps with your parents, youth pastor, small group leader, or other mature believer.

> Allow yourself some quiet space for prayer. Take a moment to realize the total lack of goodness in your life apart from Christ. Ask God to reveal to you the areas of your life in which you need the Spirit to work and produce goodness. Rest in the fact that your own goodness could never save you, but the goodness of Jesus is more than enough.

DAY 8

CAPABLE OF GOOD

- -

discover |

READ MATTHEW 7:7-12.

If you then, who are evil, know how to give good gifts
to your children, how much more will your Father in
heaven give good things to those who ask him.
—Matthew 7:11

Have you ever kept asking your parents for something? Maybe it was for a new phone, a later curfew, or just some cash to hang out with your friends. You probably get different answers at different times. Sometimes you ask and they immediately give you what you've asked for. At other times, you may ask for something and receive a firm "no." And yet at other times, they may delay their response because they know it's not the best thing for you right at that moment.

But you probably don't ask for a new phone and receive a rock; a later curfew and have them make a rule about going to bed at 4 p.m.; or cash and get some leftover printer paper. Jesus made a similar point in this parable in Matthew 7. Even though His listeners were evil, they knew how to give good gifts to their children.

You might wonder how an evil person is capable of doing anything good at all. We have all been created in God's image, which gives us the capability for good actions even though we are not naturally good because of the effect of sin on our lives. God, in His infinite goodness, gives much better gifts than what we could ever imagine.

delight

Where have you seen glimpses of goodness in our world?

What do these glimpses of goodness tell us about God's ultimate goodness?

display

We have been created in God's image. (See Gen. 1:26-27.) This image has been broken because of sin, but even that broken image reflects some of who God is. His goodness is present in the world even as broken human beings attempt to do what is right.

Make it your goal today to look for these glimpses of God's goodness. Use the notes section on pages 78-79 to write out the names of a few girls you don't really get along with or who have hurt you in the past. Beside each name, write out one glimpse of God's goodness you see in her.

Use those glimpses to point people to who God is. Maybe you'll be able to have a conversation about the gospel as you help someone connect the dots between our attempts at goodness and God's ultimate goodness.

> **Ask God to bring people into your path who need to be pointed to His goodness. Pray that He would give you eyes to see the moments when people reflect His image, even if it's a broken attempt. Thank God that His goodness is so much better than our own.**

GOD'S GOOD LOVE

- -

discover |

READ ROMANS 5:6-11.

*But God proves his own love for us in that while
we were still sinners, Christ died for us.*
—Romans 5:8

We aren't always great at sacrificing for others. We have a tendency to focus on what's best for ourselves and not spend too much effort giving up what we want so that others can benefit. Can you imagine making an intentional choice to sacrifice for a girl who doesn't even treat you well?

That's exactly what God did when He sent Jesus to die for you. It's important to realize that Jesus didn't die for you because of some sort of goodness you possess. He died for you in spite of your lack of goodness. One of the most beautiful aspects of the gospel is that Jesus made the seemingly illogical choice to die for sinners who didn't deserve it.

Jesus died for His enemies—that gives us a huge reason to celebrate and rejoice! He knew we desperately needed a Savior, and He was willing to make the ultimate sacrifice on our behalf. God reinforced His goodness and love for us through the death of Jesus, even though we didn't deserve it.

delight |

What did God do to prove His love for us?

How does this prove His love for us?

display |

It wasn't our goodness that caused Jesus to die on our behalf. It was completely an act of God's goodness. God's character moved Him to action when we didn't deserve that action. This act of love ought to motivate us to engage more intentionally in our journey to follow Jesus.

God's loving us this way also motivates us to love others who don't deserve to be loved. We don't love them because of their goodness, but instead we love them because of God's goodness and how He has extended His love to us.

List some ways you can choose to show love to the girls around you who don't tend to show love to you first.

> Thank God that He didn't wait for you to be good before sending Jesus to die for you. Sit in a quiet moment of humility as you reflect on how Jesus' dying for you was motivated by God's great goodness and love. Commit to extend that same type of love to others.

DAY 10

GOOD FOR NOTHING?

- -

discover |

READ MATTHEW 19:16-22.

Just then someone came up and asked him, "Teacher,
what good must I do to have eternal life?"
"Why do you ask me about what is good?" he said to him. "There is only
one who is good. If you want to enter into life, keep the commandments."
—Matthew 19:16–17

Earning a reward because of your hard work is a wonderful feeling—like when you put in the extra time in practice and it pays off in the game, or when you study extra and bump your grade up a notch. If we're honest, much of life works this way—except for when it comes to our goodness before God. When we try to apply that same principle of hard work to earn God's approval, it simply falls flat.

God is the only One who is good. No amount of human goodness can bring about eternal life. Jesus encountered this rich young ruler who was eager to discover how he could earn eternal life through his accomplishments. He ultimately walked away sad because, while he kept the commandments, his goodness didn't extend out to every area of his life—most clearly displayed in his love for his great wealth.

Despite the feel-good messages you might receive from the surrounding culture, you'll never be good enough on your own. True freedom comes when you stop trying to play that game. You can rest in the fact that God's goodness is the only way for you to gain eternal life.

delight |

Why do you think many people assume that their good actions will earn them eternal life?

Why are your good efforts not enough to earn God's approval?

display |

The goodness Jesus called us to is an all-in commitment. We can't make this commitment in our own strength. We need the power of the Holy Spirit to save us and transform us. Think about this: *Do you view your relationship with God as relying on your own goodness or on the goodness He provides?*

We have a tendency to let our thinking and actions be directed toward our own good and recognition. Be honest with yourself and others about your weaknesses and limitations.

In what areas of your life do you need to allow God to transform you through His goodness rather than trying to do it on your own?

> Rest in this time of prayer. Admit to God that you don't have it all together. You'll never be good enough to earn His approval. But at the same time, thank God that His goodness is enough for you. Praise Him for the eternal life He has given you.

DAY 11

GOOD SOIL

- -

discover |

READ LUKE 8:4-8,11-15.

But the seed in the good ground—these are the ones who,
having heard the word with an honest and good heart,
hold on to it and by enduring, produce fruit.
—Luke 8:15

Have your parents told you something they'd like you to do, but because you weren't really listening, you had no idea what they just said? There is a big difference between hearing and truly listening. It's one thing to hear your parents tell you take out the trash, but it's a different thing to actually listen and take out the trash.

The parable of the sower mentioned four different types of soil. Each type of soil responded differently to the seed thrown on it. The path and the rocky soil represent those who never truly listened to the Word of God or whose faith isn't rooted firmly in Him. The thorns may represent believers who just never produce fruit in their lives or people whose unbelief is revealed by their pursuit of riches and pleasure above God. The good soil, though, represents an honest and good heart that hears the Word of God, holds on to it, and endures. Ultimately, this is what produces fruit in our lives.

Do you feel like it's a struggle in your life to see spiritual fruit produced? Maybe there's some work to be done on the condition of the "soil" of your heart. God wants to speak to you through the Bible, but it's essential that you listen with a heart that's ready to receive what He has to say.

delight |

How have you observed different people responding in different ways to the message of the gospel?

What are some things that keep you from being "good soil"?

display |

It's time for a check-up on your heart. We all need the occasional check-up. The parable we've looked at today contains three key components that we see in hearts that are truly ready to hear God's Word. Pick one of these to work on today.

- The heart is honest and good. This means preparing yourself each day to hear from God in a fresh way rather than just going through the motions.

- The heart holds on to the truth it hears. Are you capturing what God says to you in a journal or some other method? Do you spend time throughout the day remembering what you've heard from God?

- The heart endures. We can't hear truth from God's Word and then do nothing with it. We must put it into practice on a consistent basis.

Ask God to reveal to you any areas of your heart that might be blocking you from truly being receptive to His Word. This might be a pattern of sin, a lack of intentional listening, or an unwillingness to put truth into action. Commit to listening with a fresh, good heart.

DAY 12

GOOD THINGS TO COME

- -

discover |

READ HEBREWS 10:1-4.

Since the law has only a shadow of the good things to come, and not the reality itself of those things, it can never perfect the worshipers by the same sacrifices they continually offer year after year.
—Hebrews 10:1

The animated classic *Peter Pan* introduces the title character in a scene in which he has lost his shadow and is searching for it in the Darling childrens' room. He chases it all over the room before finally catching it and reattaching it to himself. We laugh at the idea of a shadow being something that lives on its own. The reality is that your shadow only exists because you do.

The author of Hebrews used this imagery of a shadow when describing the Law in relationship to Jesus. The Old Testament Law was good, but it was never enough on its own. Jesus is better. He is "the good things to come." The Law is great at reminding people of their sin, but not enough to save people from their sin.

What does this mean for us today? It means all your best religious activity will never be enough to save you. At the end of the day, apart from Jesus, these efforts only point toward your need for a Savior.

delight |

What role does the Old Testament Law play in the life of a Christian?

How does knowing that the sacrifice Jesus made was permanent and enough to cover every sin you've ever committed or will commit make you feel?

display |

You may be in one of two places today with two different opportunities to live out what you've learned.

- Maybe you've never started a personal relationship with Jesus. As you read the Law discussed in the Bible, it only serves as a huge notice that you've sinned and need a Savior. If that's you, today's a great day to place your trust in Jesus and receive Him as Savior and Lord of your life.

- Or maybe you're already a follower of Jesus, but you've allowed yourself to live in a way that views following the Law as your means of earning God's approval. If that's you, reject the thinking that the law will make you righteous and remind yourself that only Jesus can do this.

Pray today that you would keep Jesus at the center of your heart and mind. Allow yourself to be reminded of your need for a Savior as you think about the sin that may have recently crept into your life. Give those sins to Jesus, because only He can forgive and bring true life.

A GOOD MAN

- -

discover |

READ ACTS 11:19-26.

For he was a good man, full of the Holy Spirit and of faith.
And large numbers of people were added to the Lord.
—Acts 11:24

What makes someone good? If only God is good, why is Barnabas described as good in Acts 11? Barnabas's goodness came not from himself, but from God. Barnabas is described as being full of the Holy Spirit and faith. So, his status as a good man is solely because of God's work in him through the Holy Spirit.

The Holy Spirit was Barnabas's source of goodness, and the result of this goodness was the encouraging and equipping of the young church at Antioch. It gave Barnabas incredible joy to see what God was doing at Antioch. He encouraged the church to stay strong in its commitment to God, and he also brought in Paul to teach and equip these new disciples.

God can do an amazing work through you when you pursue Him and desire the goodness He can bring into your life. The Lord can empower you to be characterized by goodness and can use you to encourage and equip other followers of Jesus as well. Your role is to choose daily to be filled by the Holy Spirit as you walk through life.

delight |

What are some characteristics of a good person according to the Scripture you read today?

Who is a Christian you would describe as good? What makes you describe them that way?

display |

You will never be able to live out the Christian life through your own power. It's simply impossible. Many girls struggle to walk with God because they're trying to do it on their own strength. Choose today to allow God to transform you into a person of goodness.

Is your time with God a priority in your life? Is it something you do if you end up with time in your schedule or is it part of your day no matter what happens? Explain.

One motivation to help you pursue walking with God daily is when you picture how He may use you for His kingdom work. Imagine the exciting things God wants to do through you as you encourage other believers, share the gospel with non-believers, and help other people grow in their faith.

> **Pray that God would give you a fresh desire for His goodness. Ask Him to fill you with His Spirit. Confess any times you've tried to live as a Christian on your own power. Submit your day and your desires to Him.**

A good person
produces good out
of the good stored
up in his heart. An evil
person produces evil
out of the evil stored
up in his heart, for his
mouth speaks from the
overflow of the heart.

Luke 6:45

Goodness Gracious

THE GOOD OF OTHERS

- -

discover |

READ ROMANS 15:1-6, 14.

Each one of us is to please his neighbor for his good, to build him up.
—Romans 15:2

Do you ever find yourself trying to get to the front of the line or into the front seat of the car? At times, many of us struggle with focusing on doing what's best for ourselves and not truly considering the needs of others. What you want might be good for you, but it might not be good for your friend, family member, or classmate. And in some situations, that choice might actually lead to pain and hurt in your relationships rather than the harmony God desires.

It's easy to adopt a "me first" mentality in today's culture. We are quick to look out for what's best for ourselves rather than what's truly helpful to those around us. Paul wrote to the Christians in Rome, encouraging them to put others first in the matter of which foods they felt they had the right to eat.

We don't worry too much today about which food is appropriate for us to eat, but it's critical for us to consider whether all of our actions bring good to others or only good to ourselves. God calls us to build others up by considering what is best for them, not simply what is best for us.

delight |

Have you ever made a decision that you later realized wasn't good for those around you even though it might have been good for you? How did that make you feel?

Why do you think God wants us to seek good for others?

display |

The next time you find yourself facing a decision that might affect those around you, pause. Slow down and try to see how that decision will affect the people in your life. Will it bring good to them? Or will it bring harm or difficulty? The reality is that doing something for another's good may be more difficult on you. But just because something is difficult doesn't mean it isn't the right thing to do.

Think about the girls you spend the most time with. What choices can you make today to live with their best interests at heart?

Take time to pray through any choices you may be currently facing. Ask God to give you wisdom in how those choices will affect other people. Seek to see situations the same way God does. Surrender to the Holy Spirit's control as He directs you to what is truly good for others.

LIFE IN THE LIGHT

- -

discover |

READ EPHESIANS 5:6-14.

For the fruit of the light consists of all
goodness, righteousness, and truth...
—Ephesians 5:9

Were you ever afraid of the dark? Have you seen a shape or the outline of an object in the dark and imagined it to be something sinister? Or maybe you've bumped into a wall or tripped on the stairs because just couldn't see in the dark. The funny thing is, everything changes when you turn on the light. The scary shape becomes your favorite cozy sweater stacked on the back of the chair, and you can easily avoid the wall and walk up the stairs without tripping.

Before you knew Jesus, you lived in the darkness. But now, with Jesus, you live in the light. The problem for Christians comes when they live as if they are still in darkness instead of living in the light. Walking in the light produces some key fruit: goodness, righteousness, and truth. This fruit cannot be produced while walking in darkness; it only comes from walking in the light.

There's no shame present when we walk in the light. We must simply walk in the reality that we are now children of light and not children of darkness. The result of God bringing you into the light through Jesus is a changed life. Today, you can remove the power that darkness has by focusing instead on being a child of the light.

delight |

What are some of the main differences you see between a child of darkness and a child of the light?

How have you been tempted to slip into living in the old ways of darkness?

display |

What do we do to walk in the light? First, we refuse to be deceived. It's critical to know and understand the truth God gives us through His Word. Second, we remember who we are. We are children of light. If you find yourself sliding into darkness, remind yourself of your identity as a daughter of the light. Finally, we expose the deeds of darkness instead of walking in them. The world of darkness has no power over you when you shine the light of truth on it.

On a sticky note, write out the phrase: *I am a daughter of light.* Place it where you'll see it regularly. Let this serve as a reminder of who you are and how you're called to live.

> Use your prayer time as an opportunity to reflect on your identity as a daughter of the light. Ask God to bring Scripture to mind that speaks to this new identity. Thank Him for rescuing you from the darkness. Commit to live with a new focus on your identity and not to be tempted by the darkness surrounding you in the world.

DAY 16

DESIRE FOR GOOD

- -

discover |

READ 2 THESSALONIANS 1:4-12.

*In view of this, we always pray for you that our God will make
you worthy of his calling, and by his power fulfill your every
desire to do good and your work produced by faith, so that the
name of our Lord Jesus will be glorified by you, and you by him,
according to the grace of our God and the Lord Jesus Christ.*
—2 Thessalonians 1:11-12

When you were a kid, you probably didn't like coffee (and maybe
you still don't). If you asked your parents for coffee, they probably
gave you milk or chocolate milk with just a few drops of actual
coffee. But now, grabbing coffee (or even a mocha) might have
become a regular part of your day, and maybe you even "meet for
coffee" with the girls you're closest to. Our taste in and desire for
food has a tendency to change over the years.

As followers of Jesus, our desires change as well. It may seem
completely abnormal to want to do good when you first start
growing in your faith. But as the Holy Spirit transforms your
character, you'll find that your desires change. One of those desires
is the desire to do good. But even with that new desire, it can
sometimes still be a challenge, which is why God is the One who
empowers you to be able to fulfill that desire. Today, discover how
God will provide you with the strength you need to live out this
new desire. And maybe grab a coffee.

delight |

How have you seen your desires change in a positive way since giving your life to Jesus and becoming a Christian?

Has it ever felt difficult to do good even when you wanted to? Why do you think that is?

display |

A mark of a growing Christian is an increasing desire to live God's way and to do good for others. You might need to check your heart if you are not seeing this desire increasing. Maybe there's something holding you back, like an unhealthy relationship, a sinful pattern of thinking, or even just the busyness of life. Do a quick brain dump in a journal or on a blank sheet of paper, writing out anything that comes to mind that might be holding you back. Highlight one area on your list, do some research online or using a Bible concordance, and write out what the Bible says you can do to break the hold this area has in your life.

Commit today to seek God in a fresh way as you attempt to live by His power. Don't allow yourself to fall into a pattern of trying to do good on your own. It's only possible as He gives you the desire, grows that desire, and then empowers that desire.

> Ask God to give you a fresh desire to do good. Admit your need for His power to accomplish good. Confess any times where you've tried to accomplish good on your own, apart from His strength.

DAY 17

FILLED WITH GOODNESS

- -

discover |

READ LUKE 6:43-49.

A good person produces good out of the good stored up in his heart. An evil person produces evil out of the evil stored up in his heart, for his mouth speaks from the overflow of the heart.
—Luke 6:45

Have you ever walked up to a plum tree and picked a rose? Or maybe walked up to a rose bush and picked a tulip? We all know how crazy it sounds to pick flower off a tree that doesn't match the type of tree it is. Plum trees grow plums and rose bushes grow roses.

In the same way, good people produce good fruit and bad people produce bad fruit. The key to producing good fruit in our lives isn't found in trying harder. The good fruit comes from our lives when our hearts are filled with goodness through the Holy Spirit.

So how does someone become filled with goodness? Jesus illustrated this when He talked about building your life on a solid foundation of rock. The solid foundation comes when you take what Jesus taught and actually put it into practice. Jesus isn't looking for followers who simply hear what He says. He's looking for followers who will do what He says.

delight |

What do you think are some examples of fruit that are produced from the life of a good person?

How have you seen God produce fruit through your life?

display |

The most important thing you can focus on in life is developing a heart that's committed to Jesus's teachings and obeying them.

Take a deep look inside your heart, and as you reflect on the type of fruit that comes out of your life, write out your thoughts in the notes section on pages 78-79. What does the fruit of your life look like? Is it fruit that points people to Jesus or points them away from Him?

We have to know Jesus' teachings to obey them. Spend time every day reading at least a little bit of the Bible. Ask God each day to give you insight into His Word. As you get to know these teachings better, commit to living them out by your actions throughout the day. Then, you'll be filled with goodness through the power of the Holy Spirit.

What main insight did you gain from your reading today?

> Spend a few moments in reflective prayer. Ask God to show you what the true state of your heart is. Ask Him to reveal areas that need to line up more with who He's calling you to be. Surrender to all that God asks you to do, and commit to live out His teachings with a good heart today.

DAY 18

DO WHAT IS GOOD

- -

discover |

READ 1 PETER 3:8-12.

*For the one who wants to love life and to see good days, let
him keep his tongue from evil and his lips from speaking
deceit, and let him turn away from evil and do what is good.
Let him seek peace and pursue it, because the eyes of the Lord
are on the righteous and his ears are open to their prayer. But
the face of the Lord is against those who do what is evil.*
— 1 Peter 3:10-12

Life is full of "if/then" situations. If you drive over the speed limit,
then you will get a ticket. If you leave cookies in the oven too long,
then they will burn and taste terrible. If you don't study for your
math test, then your grade will suffer.

Today's passage contains a similar situation. If you do what is good,
then God will have His eyes on you and hear your prayer. If you
do what is evil, then His face will be against you. It's important to
note that our approval before God comes only through Jesus, but
because of our new life in Christ, the result is righteousness and
God's response as described here.

The passage also gives a simple list of what to do and what not to
do. The life of a good person is marked by things like sympathy
and love for one another. The life of an evil person is marked by
things like insulting others when they insult you. Our goal should
be to live in goodness as God tells us through His Word.

delight |

How would you describe the differences between the actions of a good person and an evil person?

What does it look like for you to turn away from evil and do what is good?

display |

The good person's life is marked by doing no evil. Here's what happens as you continue to grow in your walk with Jesus: you'll discover a greater desire to do good and a greater hatred of doing what's evil. Don't hear this wrong. You will always wrestle with temptation, but you will find an ever-increasing desire to do what's good the deeper your relationship goes with Jesus.

Have you been allowing evil into parts of your life? In the notes section on pages 78-79, write out anything that comes to mind. Decide today to take a turn in the opposite direction. Choose what's good instead of what's evil. Next to each allowance of evil, write out one way you can do what is good instead. Remember that God is ready to hear your prayers as you continue to pursue Him.

> Meditate on the actions Peter described, both good and evil. Ask God to show you an area to either begin pursuing or to turn away from. Commit that area to the Lord as He gives you the strength to make a change.

LOVE YOUR ENEMIES

- -

discover |

READ MATTHEW 5:43-48.

But I tell you, love your enemies and pray for those who persecute you, so that you may be children of your Father in heaven. For he causes his sun to rise on the evil and the good, and sends rain on the righteous and the unrighteous.
—Matthew 5:44–45

It's easy to love people who are nice to you. No great feat is accomplished when you act loving toward your friends and the girls who treat you well. It isn't hard to show love to your brother or sister when they're being kind. But it is difficult to love girls who are mean or rude. These are girls you might even think of as enemies.

Jesus flipped the common understanding of what it meant to love your neighbor. People at that time understood it to be about loving your neighbor but hating your enemy. If we claim to be children of God, then we must love our enemies in the same way He has loved His enemies. In fact, He loved you while you were still in sin and an enemy of God.

As you think today about what it means to love your enemy, keep in mind that love isn't about a feeling. Loving someone means you do good to them. It's actively choosing to do what's best for someone else, even if they don't do it back.

delight |

What is your natural response when someone treats you badly?

Why do you think Jesus made such a big deal about loving our enemies?

display |

The call to love your enemies is one of the most challenging commands Jesus gives us. But at the same time, it's one of the clearest ways we can see God transforming our character to look more like Jesus. There's probably a girl in your life that you might consider to be an enemy. Choose today to do good toward your enemy. Choose to love her when she's unloving. Choose to be a reflection of the love our Father has shown toward us.

What's one way you can do good for this girl today, to show her love no matter what she's done to you?

It's easy to pray for people you care deeply about, but it's tough to pray for people who are tough to love. Next time you find yourself frustrated with a girl you know, you might be tempted to complain about her or vent your frustrations. Instead, pray for her. You'll discover quickly that praying for your enemies transforms the way you feel about them and act toward them.

> Take a few minutes to pray specifically for people who are tough to love. Pray for them by name. Ask God to bring blessings into their lives. Commit to loving people even when they may not love you back.

AUTHENTIC GOODNESS

- -

discover |

READ MATTHEW 22:1-14.

"Go then to where the roads exit the city and invite everyone
you can to the banquet." So those servants went out on
the roads and gathered everyone they found, both evil and
good. The wedding banquet was filled with guests.
—Matthew 22:9-10

Everyone loves a good story. There's nothing better than hearing a great storyteller bring things to life through his or her words. Jesus was a master storyteller and often used parables as a way to communicate spiritual truths.

In Matthew 22:1-14, Jesus gave a picture of the people of Israel— God's chosen people. God had sent His messengers to them, but the people of Israel rejected these messengers. Jesus described God's judgment on those who rejected the message. The Father broadly opened up the invitation to all people to be His chosen people, no matter their goodness before knowing Him.

The picture of a full wedding banquet is incredible, but it also came with a warning. One guest in the parable wasn't wearing the proper wedding clothes. He was thrown out and punished. You can't fake a relationship with God. You may be able to fool your friends, your pastor, and even your parents, but you will never be able to fool God. He provides the proper wedding clothes by allowing each of us the opportunity to place our trust in Christ.

delight |

Why do you think the guests who were initially invited to the wedding responded the way they did?

How does our goodness show that we truly belong to God?

display |

You can never earn your way to salvation. There's no amount of religious ritual or good deeds that could earn God's approval. This is evident in today's passage when we see the guest who was not properly dressed for the wedding. You might be tempted to "fake it until you make it," but God sees through our attempts to appear to be something we are not.

The goodness your life displays is a gift from God. It shows that you belong to Him. Seek to live your life in a way that is grateful for how God has invited you to the greatest wedding banquet of all time. In the notes section on pages 78-79, list some ideas of ways you can live gratefully this week.

> Express a prayer of gratitude today. Thank God for including you in His invitation to know Him. Praise Him for including you in His chosen people. Remind yourself that it's only because of God's open invitation that you can have the privilege of knowing Him now.

DAY 21

GOODNESS DOES

- -

discover |

READ MATTHEW 25:14-30.

*"His master said to him, 'Well done, good and faithful
servant! You were faithful over a few things; I will put you
in charge of many things. Share your master's joy.'"*
—Matthew 25:21

That little jolt you get inside when someone congratulates you
for a job well done is one of the best feelings. It's like getting the
top grade on an assignment, hearing applause as you finish your
solo, or cooking a great meal for your family. Can you imagine how
incredible it would feel to hear God tell you that you've done a
good job?

God gives different gifts, abilities, and resources to every Christian.
The main point here isn't about how much He's given you, but
rather what you do with what you've been given. Do you have a
talent for singing? You can use your gifts to lead others in worship.
Are you good with kids? You can use that gift to help a single
parent who can't afford childcare. The key is using what God has
given you for His glory and helping to accomplish His mission.

On the flip side, Jesus used strong words in this parable for the
servant who simply hid away what he received. This servant was
described as wicked and lazy. The end result for that service (or
lack thereof) was the opposite of what you hope to hear when
everything is said and done. We are called to be servants who are
active in doing good through what God has given to us.

delight |

Why did the last servant simply hide his gift away?

What keeps you from fully using the gifts God has given you?

display |

Good and faithful. Aren't those two words you'd love to hear when you see Jesus face-to-face one day? This response is based on what you do now. God has gifted you. He's given you a unique personality, abilities, life experience, and spiritual gifts, and He doesn't want you to waste them.

Be a Christian who puts her faith into action. You've been placed for a purpose in this particular place and at this particular time. God has gifted you so you can use those gifts.

Write out a list of the ways you know God has gifted you. Next to each one, write out at least one idea for a way to use that gift for God's glory.

> Pray that God would help you see clearly how He has gifted and equipped you for a purpose. Commit to discovering those gifts and putting them to good use. Ask God to give you a clear opportunity to glorify Him by putting your gifts into action.

NOT A MATCH

- -

discover |

READ MATTHEW 25:31-46.

"Then he will also say to those on the left, 'Depart from me,
you who are cursed, into the eternal fire prepared for the devil
and his angels! For I was hungry and you gave me nothing to
eat; I was thirsty and you gave me nothing to drink; I was a
stranger and you didn't take me in; I was naked and you didn't
clothe me, sick and in prison and you didn't take care of me.'"
—Matthew 25:41–43

In the Scripture for today, Jesus continued the theme from earlier in Matthew 25. He highlighted how people who took care of those in need were actually taking care of Him. However, the opposite was also true. Those who didn't care for others in need had actually neglected Jesus. He referred to this second group of people as goats.

This passage gives us some insight into the earlier part of Matthew 25. Why did the man who buried the one talent get cast out? He was like the goats in today's passage. He looked the part of a believer, but he clearly didn't believe. His life and actions didn't match up with what he'd said.

A true Christ follower is known by her actions. God's goodness overflows through her as she loves people others might overlook. We point others toward Jesus when we live out what we say we believe.

delight |

Why did Jesus tell the people to depart from Him (vv. 41-43)? How do you think the people felt when they heard these words from Jesus?

Why is it so important that our actions match our beliefs?

display |

God's goodness is designed to show up in the way we live. The natural response for a believer when she sees a hurting person is to do whatever she can to meet that need. God has a huge heart for people the world sees as the least. God is calling you to have that same heart and love.

You can discover all sorts of ways to minister to people who are hurting. You can ask your parents to go with you to visit sick people from your church, get some friends together to serve in a local homeless shelter in your city, or maybe you can collect canned food to give to people who are in need. The bottom line is this: Christians see needs and seek to meet them.

How will you meet the needs you see today? List a few ideas.

During your time of prayer, ask God to give you a bigger heart for the least, the lost, and the left out. Seek His direction for how to personally get involved with helping those who need ministry in this way. Ask for open eyes to see the needs you might overlook every day.

EAGER TO DO GOOD

- -

discover |

READ TITUS 2:11-14.

He gave himself for us to redeem us from all lawlessness and to cleanse for himself a people for his own possession, eager to do good works.
—Titus 2:14

You probably have some responsibilities at home that you don't exactly enjoy. Maybe it's taking out the trash, cleaning the bathrooms, or unloading the dishwasher. In fact, if you acted overly excited about any of those tasks, the rest of your family might look at you like you were crazy. Can you imagine being excited about doing chores around the house?

But that's exactly what God calls us to when it comes to doing good works. We shouldn't serve in ministry or help people out just because it's what we're supposed to do. Instead, we should have an attitude of eagerness when it comes to doing those things. Imagine jumping at the opportunity to serve and do good for others.

God has rescued you through Christ, not just so that you can be free from sin, but so you would be eager to do good works. He's creating a people who find absolute joy in the act of serving others and putting others' needs before their own.

delight |

What has God instructed us to avoid because of our salvation (v. 12)?

What has God commanded us to do in the place of the things to avoid (v. 12)?

display |

You weren't saved so you could just sit, attend church, and be with other Christians. Those things are important, but the purpose of your salvation is much bigger than that. You've been called to develop a heart that's eager to do good works.

On a scale of one to ten, how eager are you to do good works?

1   2   3   4   5   6   7   8   9   10

Nope.   **Meh.**   **For sure!**

It's easy to sometimes get into a rut of doing good just because it's what we're supposed to do out of some sense of duty. The next time you help someone out or serve in ministry, ask God to give you a fresh sense of eagerness. Spend time thinking about your attitude as you serve. If change is needed, decide to start developing the heart you know God wants you to have.

> **Praise God for the gift of salvation. Thank Him for what He's saved you from. Ask Him to remind you that He saved you for good works. If your attitude toward good works hasn't been great, ask God to give you a renewed sense of eagerness to do good works.**

Therefore, brothers and sisters, in view of the mercies of God, I urge you to present your bodies as a living sacrifice, holy and pleasing to God; this is your true worship.

Do not be conformed to this age, but be transformed by the renewing of your mind, so that you may discern what is the good, pleasing, and perfect will of God.

ROMANS 12:1–2

DAY 24

THREE GOOD THINGS

- -

discover |

READ MICAH 6:8.

*Mankind, he has told each of you what is good and
what it is the LORD requires of you: to act justly, to love
faithfulness, and to walk humbly with your God.*

Imagine you got a job working at a local coffee shop. (Maybe you
already have one!) They'll spend some time teaching you how to
work the equipment and the proper way to interact with customers.
Chances are, they'll give you a job description—a written list of
what's expected of you as an employee. Wouldn't it be great if all
of life had a list of expectations like this?

In Micah 6:8, we're given three simple tasks that fulfill what God
requires of us as His people. We're called to:

- act justly. This means treating others fairly, telling the truth,
  and speaking out on behalf of those who can't speak
  for themselves.
- love faithfulness. God calls you to faithfully obey Him
  in all His commands, showing your heart's commitment
  to faithfulness.
- walk humbly with God. Our walk is a close relationship with
  God, but we also need to pursue it in humility. A humble
  walk means keeping a clear view of who God is and who
  you are in relationship to Him.

Even though these seem simple, there's much to explore here. You
just might discover an area where you need to do some growing.

delight |

Which of these three commands is the most difficult for you? Why?

Which of the three comes easiest for you? Why?

display |

Act justly. Love faithfulness. Walk humbly with your God. These three simple expectations summarize what it looks like to follow God. Even though they're simple, it will take you an entire lifetime to explore what it really means to live these out. As you live out these commands, people will see a difference in your life. A changed life points people to Jesus.

Think about your life. How's your walk? List a few ideas of how can you live out these three qualities today.

Take a few minutes of quiet prayer. Ask God to show you how to live out this verse in your life. Repent of any areas where you haven't been living it out. Commit to growing in each of these areas.

DAY 25

KNOW WHAT IS GOOD

- -

discover |

READ ROMANS 12:1-2.

Therefore, brothers and sisters, in view of the mercies of God, I urge you to present your bodies as a living sacrifice, holy and pleasing to God; this is your true worship. Do not be conformed to this age, but be transformed by the renewing of your mind, so that you may discern what is the good, pleasing, and perfect will of God.

What do you picture when you hear the word *worship*? You might picture things like a church service, singing, or maybe reading Scripture. All of those things are absolutely a part of worship, but worship is actually much bigger than that. Paul told the church in Rome that worship is actually about presenting ourselves as a living sacrifice.

A sacrifice in the Bible was typically an animal that was killed and offered to God. But a living sacrifice goes even further. A girl who is seeks to be a living sacrifice has to make a daily choice to surrender to God's way instead of her own way. A girl who is a living sacrifice isn't influenced by culture, but is instead transformed by a changed, or renewed, mind.

As you continue in this process of transformation, you're able to see clearly the good, pleasing, and perfect will of God. If you need clarity with a decision, the first place to start is by allowing your mind to be changed into God's way of thinking. In your time here today, start this process of transformation as you dig into God's Word.

delight |

What should motivate you to this "true worship"?

How can you allow God to renew your mind and transform you?

display |

Everyone wants to know God's will for their lives, but it's not as mysterious as you might think. The key to knowing God's will starts with changing the way you think and see things. The process of being a living sacrifice daily and being transformed daily allows you to see God's point of view much more clearly. You won't ever understand everything, but you'll be able to know what good things to do next.

Here are a couple of questions for you: Are you regularly being a living sacrifice? Are you regularly allowing God to renew your mind? It won't happen apart from spending time in the Bible and prayer. Carve out time each day for this important process. In the margin of your Bible or on your Bible app, make a note by today's passage that says: *I commit to allowing myself to be transformed and renewed every day through Scripture and prayer.*

> Focus on the idea of surrender. A living sacrifice requires giving up your own desires and replacing them with God's desires. Surrender to His will rather than your flesh. Surrender to God's way of thinking instead of your own. Ask God to renew your mind daily so you can be transformed.

DAY 26

IMITATE THE GOOD

- -

discover |

READ 3 JOHN 1:11.

Dear friend, do not imitate what is evil, but what is good. The one
who does good is of God; the one who does evil has not seen God.

Have you ever shopped at a thrift store or hunted for the best sales
and ended up with a dress or sweater from some brand you've
never heard of? While it might not be the name brand everyone
seems to be wearing, you can usually find items that look like the
real deal. And you walk away paying a fraction of the cost!

Imitation sounds like a bad thing to us sometimes, but the reality
is, we all imitate things around us even if we hate to admit it. In
3 John, the apostle encouraged us to think carefully about what we
imitate. It's quick and easy to imitate what's evil because it's what
we see around us in the world all day. It takes intentional effort to
imitate what's good.

If you want to know a girl's true character, look at whether she
consistently imitates evil or good. None of us are perfect, and we
all will sin at times. But the pattern of our lives ought to be one of
choosing to imitate good, showing that we truly belong to God.

delight |

What might a person's life look like if she primarily imitates evil?

What might a person's life look like if she primarily imitates good?

display |

To figure out what imitating good looks like, we have to start with Scripture. The Bible is full of instruction and examples of how to imitate what is good. It can also be a good idea to connect with a godly girl or woman who has been following Jesus a little while longer than you have. It's helpful to see faith lived out in real life so you can imitate it.

Who comes to mind when you consider other girls and women you can imitate?

The next step of imitating good is realizing that other girls look to your life to figure out what imitating good looks like. As you grow in your faith, look for a younger girl that you can help grow in her faith. You won't be the only example in her life, but you can be one important person who helps her see what it looks like to follow Jesus in a meaningful way.

Who comes to mind when you think about a girl you can influence?

> Pray that God would open your eyes to what the Bible says about imitating good. Ask God to show you mentors in your life who can help you see how to live out the Bible's teachings. Surrender your heart to God as He prepares you to be an influence in others' lives.

CLING TO GOOD, PART 1

- -

discover |

READ ROMANS 12:9-10.

Let love be without hypocrisy. Detest evil; cling to what is good.
—Romans 12:9

You've probably met a girl who tried to be loving and friendly, but came across as fake. She smiled to your face and maybe even told you it was great to see you, but you still picked up on something being off. Paul challenged us to love without hypocrisy. In other words, our love for others should be an authentic, honest, and open type of love. This kind of love is the opposite of evil.

The apostle Paul often gave a good replacement when he told us to avoid bad behavior. The replacement behavior here for detesting evil is to cling to what is good. In the context of this passage, this is lived out in our love for others. We're to love one another in a deep way, like brothers and sisters. As a Christian, your spiritual family takes on an importance similar to the family you're born into.

We love others deeply primarily in the way we treat them. We're to honor one another, too. This type of honor requires putting others' needs above our own, treating people with respect, and always assuming the best in them.

delight |

What does it look like to love without hypocrisy?

Why is it important to view other Christians as our brothers and sisters?

display |

Evil and good are complete opposites of each other. You can't be pursuing what is good while slightly dabbling in what is evil. That's why Paul made it so clear that we are to detest evil and cling to good. "Detest" is another word for hate. How is your hatred of evil? We're not necessarily talking about evil in others, but in you.

How much do you hate it when you give in to sin?

1	2	3	4	5	6	7	8	9	10

Not at all.   **Kind of.**   **Loathe entirely.**

On that same note, how are you doing at clinging to what is good? Clinging to what is good is more than acting a certain way at church and another way at school. Picture a girl clinging to the side of a cliff while rock climbing. She'll use every ounce of her energy to cling on to what she can. Your pursuit of good should have that same type of intensity.

List three ways you can cling to what is good as you interact with others today.

> Ask God to give you an ever-increasing desire to cling to what is good. Repent of any times you've dabbled with evil rather than detesting it. Pray that God would show you opportunities to love others deeply.

Goodness Gracious

CLING TO GOOD, PART 2

- -

discover |

READ ROMANS 12:11-15.

Do not lack diligence in zeal; be fervent in the Spirit; serve the Lord.
—*Romans 12:11*

The process of clinging to what is good is essential for us to grow in our walk with God. In today's passage, Paul gave a series of short commands that really help us figure out what it looks like to cling to good.

- **Be fervent in the Spirit.** Paul encouraged Christians to have a passion and enthusiasm for their faith. People get enthusiastic about their favorite singer, restaurant, or hobby. But what if that same level of enthusiasm was directed by the Holy Spirit? This type of enthusiasm would be centered on the things of God rather than the things of this world.

- **Serve the Lord.** Walking in the Spirit enthusiastically will always lead to a passion to serve God. Your faith needs to have a place to flow out of your life and not just be in a constant state of receiving. If you find that you don't have a desire to serve the Lord, maybe it's time to reexamine your walk with God and reconnect with Him in a fresh way.

Look closely at the other short commands Paul gave in this passage. You'll find encouragement there to pray, rejoice, share, and more. Each of these is a critical part of clinging to good.

delight |

Take a look through the list of commands in this passage. Which one do you need to work on most?

Who can help you grow in that command? Which commands can you help others grow to obey? Who could you help now?

display |

The process of clinging to good is completely tied to the resulting actions in our lives. In other words, as you cling to what is good, it will change the way you live and treat other people. It's difficult to bless those who persecute you. It's challenging to be patient in affliction. It's not always easy to be hospitable to others. But the life of a follower of Jesus is marked by these things. It's both the result of clinging to good and the process of learning to cling to good.

Put these commands into practice even if you don't feel like it. Create new habits of how you treat others that will ultimately shape your life and character.

Write out two practical ways you can create new habits today.

Focus on one or two of the commands in this passage and ask God for His help in living them out. Confess your need for His strength as you recognize you can't do this alone.

DAY 29

CLING TO GOOD, PART 3

- -

discover |

READ ROMANS 12:16-18.

If possible, as far as it depends on you, live at peace with everyone.
—Romans 12:18

Here's the thing: You can neither predict nor control others' actions. You are not responsible for what they choose to do, but you are responsible for how you choose to respond. This can be especially tough when you're hurt, confused, or feel completely blindsided by someone else's actions. Still, you can go into every situation prepared if you choose to remain focused on acting and responding in a God-honoring way. Sometimes, responding with kindness is all you need to diffuse a potentially tense situation.

In continuing our theme of clinging to good, Paul gave a great piece of wisdom: We're to live at peace with everyone. But he also included an important note here: "as far as it depends on you." Maybe there's a girl who has been treating you poorly. You can't fix what she has done, but you can choose to treat her with kindness and to not stir up any more issues.

Think about the part you play in keeping harmony in the different relationships in your life. You can't control everything that happens, but you can make some key choices that will help you live at peace with everyone.

delight |

Why is it not always possible to live at peace with everyone?

What are some ways you think Christians can make a better effort to live at peace with everyone?

display |

You do not have complete control over the health of every relationship you're in. You really don't have any control over how other people act in relationships. But you do have control over how you act in relationships and how you respond to conflict.

How do you respond when a friend or family member treats you poorly? Do you blow up in anger? Do you retreat and get silent? Think about your most recent reactions. Describe your go-to response in a journal or on a blank sheet of paper. How can you shift your typical reaction to respond with God's love as best as you can instead? Don't forget that you have the Holy Spirit living in you, and He will empower you to love people as God wants you to.

Ask God to reveal relationships to you which may need to make a greater effort to live at peace. Confess any ways you may have contributed to the conflict in the relationship. Commit to approaching those relationships differently.

DAY 30

CONQUER EVIL WITH GOOD

- -

discover |

READ ROMANS 12:19-21.

Do not be conquered by evil, but conquer evil with good.
—Romans 12:21

You've probably heard the saying, "Don't get mad. Get even." This is terrible advice! Our natural reaction when someone hurts us is to get back at them. We may even want to hurt them slightly worse than they hurt us. This type of approach never ends well.

Paul made clear in this passage that vengeance, or getting back at someone, is not your job. Vengeance belongs to God. You must remember that God will one day set everything right that has been made wrong. So when we choose to return evil with evil, we're forgetting our place in the big picture. Our role isn't to bring punishment on others. God will determine where judgment is needed and what it will look like.

Instead of repaying evil with evil, you can choose a completely different approach. Paul said your approach ought to be repaying evil with good. This approach makes no sense in our culture. We want to get back at people when they hurt us. Instead, Christians are commanded to simply bring blessings upon people when they hurt us.

Today, determine to hear these words of Scripture with fresh ears. Listen to what God is saying through Paul. You may find some relationships in your life where you've been hoping for revenge, but can now choose a different approach.

delight |

Why is it important to recognize that vengeance belongs to God instead of us?

What is one way you can choose to conquer evil with good?

display |

The act of seeking vengeance when you're hurt is never helpful. It may make you feel good in the moment, but it doesn't really accomplish anything. Plus, it tries to take over God's role in the situation. Think through relationships in your life where there may be some difficulties. Have you been trying to seek revenge in any of them? If so, how can you choose to love and bless them instead? Write out a few ideas in the notes section on pages 78-79.

It's tough to not seek revenge. The easy choice is to go for the cheap shot and seek vengeance on your own. Make the difficult choice to trust that God will do what's right when others have harmed you. This choice will be the best choice for both you and the person who hurt you.

> Take a few minutes in quiet prayer. If there are any relationships where someone has caused you hurt, now is the time to release that hurt. Give that hurt and pain to God instead of carrying it yourself. Surrender the desire to seek revenge and tell God of your trust in Him with all relationships in your life.

A DIFFERENT KIND OF GOOD

How do we know that God is good? We sing about His goodness, we read in His Word that He is good, and when troubling situations arise, we often hear people say, "But God is still good!" While all of these things are true, have you ever stopped to think about what it really means to say that God is good?

Describe what you mean when you say God is good or what you think when you hear someone else say God is good.

Maybe some of our uncertainty over the question of "Is God good?" can be attributed to the overuse and misunderstanding of the word in general. When we think "good," we might think: "Well, it's so-so, but it's isn't awesome." Or we may think of good as something that is favorable, thriving, attractive, unharmed/OK, sound, not expired, pleasant, or witty.[1]

How would you describe your standard for good?

When you think about God being good, does this come from your own personal standard for good? Or do you believe God exists above and beyond what we could define as good? Explain.

Read Exodus 33; 34:6; Nehemiah 9:20; Psalm 27:13; 145:9; Mark 10:18; and James 1:17. What would you change about your definition of God's goodness after reading these verses? Why?

Here's the thing: God isn't "good" by comparison to something or someone else. He isn't good because He lives up to (or obliterates) our personal standards for goodness. His goodness isn't harsh, uncaring, or any other negative argument people make against God's goodness. It's not even His holiness, mercy, or ethical standard—though those things are true.

God's goodness flows from His character as the one true God, who is never in need, but, instead, constantly gives to the ones He created. His goodness encompasses His kindness, generosity, and the overall joy He brings to the world He so deeply loves. His goodness is necessary because it is a part of His character. But He doesn't have to be good to us—He chooses to. And God wants us to know Him and enjoy His goodness! He expresses this time and time again in His Word and in His actions.[2]

Think about it: God loves us so deeply and so intensely desires us to experience His goodness that our holy God made a way for a sinful world to be forgiven. And the way wasn't painless, but required the sacrifice of His only Son to bring death to sin and victory over the grave so that we might have a relationship with Him. Every second, He extends an invitation for us to come and enjoy "the LORD's goodness in the land of the living" (Ps. 27:13).

Describe how your definition of God's goodness has changed throughout this devotional.

BEFORE I STARTED

AFTER I FINISHED

I KNEW ALL ALONG

WHAT IT TAKES TO BE GOOD

As we know, everyone has a different definition of what's "good," so it should come as no surprise that the idea of what makes a person good varies, too. While you may be ready to spout off the church answer of "It's Jesus," just hold onto that thought for a minute. While that answer is correct, have you ever considered the backing for it? Do you know how to support the idea that Jesus is the ONLY thing that makes us good in a sinful culture filled with competing ideas about what "good" really is?

Let's start by taking a look at some common cultural beliefs about what it means to be "good." Then, we'll take a look at what God's Word says is true. For each option, color, shade, or highlight the icon that most accurately represents your view: thumbs up icon (if you agree) or the thumbs down icon (if you disagree).

You're a good person if …

 1. **You're a rule follower. You don't steal or cheat, and you try to always tell the truth.**

2. **You have a "moral compass" and you stick to your beliefs while respecting others.**

3. **Those closest to you—your friends, family, small group members, classmates, and so on—can describe you as someone who has solid character.**

4. **You're not arrogant or too stuck on yourself. You're compassionate and considerate of others.**

5. **You're neither too objective nor too emotional. You look at all the facts before making a decision, but you balance that by considering feelings, too.[3]**

How do these statements align with what you already know about God, His Word, His goodness, and His plan for us?

Truthfully, Scripture describes us—humanity as a whole—as sinful. But what does that mean?

- *Merriam-Webster* defines sin as "an offense against religious or moral law; an action that is or is felt to be highly reprehensible; an often serious shortcoming."[4]

- The *Holman Illustrated Bible Dictionary* says that sin is any action "by which humans rebel against God, miss His purpose for their life, and surrender to the power of evil rather than to God."[5]

Put simply, sin is unrighteousness or going against God's good design for us. Even though the cultural definition doesn't say that explicitly, the actions listed as sin are still not God's best for us. These definitions reveal what is "bad" or wrong, but both also clearly point to what they believe to be the solution:

- Don't disobey the religious/moral law you follow. Don't do anything that others would find worthy of judgment. Work on ironing out your flaws.

- Follow God and His Word. Pursue His purpose for your life. Give your life fully to Him.

From our culture's vantage point, we are in control—we just need to work on being the best version of ourselves, whatever that happens to be in the court of popular opinion. From a biblical perspective, we are completely unable to make ourselves good because we are sinful and unrighteous. But the good news is that God is able to make us good—He provided a way for us to be made holy and righteous through Jesus.

The world tells us we're good by what we do and based on our character, but God says we're good because of what He's done for us and based on His character. So, we are not saved because we are good. We are saved because He is good. We are saved from ourselves, for Him (to be His children), and for the good works He has planned for us.

A MEASURE OF GOOD

Briefly review the actions our culture says make someone a good person on pages 74-75, then take a few minutes to complete the following. Rate how "good" each action is on a scale of 1 to 10, with one being "nothing good here," five being "eh, anyone would do that," and 10 being "wow, that's amazing!"

Maddie does her best to refrain from gossip, foul language, and making suggestive jokes.

1   2   3   4   5   6   7   8   9   10

Alina tries not to put herself in situations where she's alone with a guy and keeps parental locks on her phone and computer so she doesn't see graphic images.

1   2   3   4   5   6   7   8   9   10

Instead of going out with friends on Friday nights, Leilani helps provide childcare at her church for attendees of an addiction recovery program.

1   2   3   4   5   6   7   8   9   10

At least once a week, Sofía's mom takes her to visit with an elderly widow from her church. They spend hours together, baking cookies and talking about life.

1   2   3   4   5   6   7   8   9   10

Keisha donates her old clothes, shoes, and purses to a clothing closet in her community that provides for the poor.

1   2   3   4   5   6   7   8   9   10

Although each of these are good—and biblical (see Prov. 1:17; 1 Cor. 6:18; Phil. 2:4; Eph. 4:29-31; and Jas. 1:27)—things we can do for others, the actions in and of themselves are not good or what make us good. They aren't what save us, either. We've already discussed God's goodness and what it means for us to be "good," but we have to take a deeper look at what it means to be saved for good works, not by them.

We frequently hear the mantra in our culture of "You are enough." As an encouragement to be who God created you to be, and that you don't have to be and do everything, this holds up. But it doesn't quite translate into our spiritual lives. The harsh reality here is that we could never measure up to God's standard of holiness or be "good enough" on our own. Thankfully, alongside this difficult truth is a grace beyond our comprehension: Jesus' perfect life and sacrifice for us was, is, and always will be good enough.

We don't have to be perfect to have a relationship with God, we just have to have Jesus.

Notes

sources

1 "Good," accessed March 23, 2021, https://www.merriam-webster.com/dictionary/good.

2 Kevin DeYoung, "The Goodness of God," The Gospel Coalition, April 20, 2020, https://www.thegospelcoalition.org/blogs/kevin-deyoung/the-goodness-of-god/.

3 Ronald E Riggio, "How Can You Tell If You Are a Good Person?," Psychology Today (Sussex Publishers, October 14, 2016), https://www.psychologytoday.com/blog/cutting-edge-leadership/201610/how-can-you-tell-if-you-are-good-person?eml.

4 "Sin," Merriam-Webster (Merriam-Webster), accessed March 25, 2021, https://www.merriam-webster.com/dictionary/sin.

5 Chad Brand et al., "Sin," in *Holman Illustrated Bible Dictionary* (Nashville, TN: Holman Reference, 2015).